THE BOOK OF FAILURES

poems

Also by Neil Shepard:

How It Is: Selected Poems (2018)

Vermont Exit Ramps II (2016)

Hominid Up (2015)

Vermont Exit Ramps I (2012)

Travel/Untravel (2011)

This Far from the Source (2006)

I'm Here Because I Lost My Way (1998)

Scavenging the Country for a Heartbeat (1993)

THE BOOK OF FAILURES

poems

Neil Shepard

MADVILLE
PUBLISHING

LAKE DALLAS, TEXAS

Copyright © 2024 by Neil Shepard
All rights reserved
Printed in the United States of America

FIRST EDITION

Requests for permission to reprint or reuse material from this work should be sent to:

Permissions
Madville Publishing
PO Box 358
Lake Dallas, TX 75065

Author Photo: Scott Pasfield
Cover Design: Anna Riley-Shepard

ISBN: 978-1-956440-69-0 paperback
978-1-956440-70-6 ebook
Library of Congress Control Number: 2023942794

for my father (1921-2017)
and my mother (1925-2023)

CONTENTS

I

1   Milk, Eggs, Bread
3   End of August
4   Horses Standing in Rain
5   Late Fall
6   Under the Radar
7   Spring Poem, NYC
9   And Why Not Be Happy
11   Exiles
12   In the Vilnius Café
13   Going for a Drive
14   Dad's Been Crying Again
16   After the Blizzard
18   The Wasting

II

31   Seagull in a Bowl
32   Rodin's *Le Baiser*
33   Cezanne's Atelier
35   Great Cities
36   The Band's Visit
38   Waves Going Out, Waves Coming In,
39   Mating Behaviors of Storks, Egrets, Humans
41   Local Freeze
42   Questions for a Cormorant
43   Cormorants in Full Sun
45   Big Winds
46   So What
47   Peacocks, for Evans

49	That Sad Clapping
51	Like Blue Behind a Daytime Moon
53	How She Got That Voice
54	There Is No Sadness
55	Finifugal

III

59	Lines Written at Tyrone Guthrie
67	Staigue Fort
68	Worth
69	Lockdown in La Ciotat
87	Crows in Snow
88	Grudging Spring
90	Acknowledgments
91	About the Author

I

MILK, EGGS, BREAD

I keep thinking of John Sullivan,
not the famous John L. Sullivan
in *Sullivan's Travels*, who
made film's first tragic
comedy, nor the famous
boxer, John L. Sullivan, the world's
first heavyweight champion,
nor the scarcely less famous
John L. Sullivan, the boxing
elephant with Barnum & Bailey.
No, I keep thinking of
John Sullivan, the small-
town selectman, who, when
our group suggested new
signage at the edge of the village
to advertise our strengths—
education, arts, industry—
he said, in jest, I suppose, *Why
not 'milk, eggs, bread'?*
to which I was mightily
offended, having sat up nights
penning that very phrase—
education, arts, industry—
though, I admit, I couldn't
think of 'industry,' at the time,
there being nothing
but long-gone mills,
and, somehow, just
two proud nouns—
'education, arts'
(for the state college
and the arts colony
in the rural backwater)—
just wouldn't do,
so I fudged the third,

'industry,' with a back-
ward glance to our founding
past, which led, I guess,
to John Sullivan's famous
wisecrack, famous,
at least, for me.
And yet, why not
'milk, eggs, bread,' those staples
that sustain us in a small town
and keep us from each other's
throats and larders, as after
the heated meeting, John
invited me home to break
bread together of an evening
meal, and we made the small
talk by which we live and
suffer and endure, and next
Saturday morning, I called
across the fence for him
to come over and share
scrambled eggs, toast, and
a cold glass of milk.

END OF AUGUST

Brittle, blond grasses of a pasture
That's gone uncut, unproductive all summer.
I've called and called, but the young farmer
Says he's got better-yield fields to mow and bale.
Now he arrives to say my crappy hay
Will fetch a lousy sales price; it's full
Of vetch and bedstraw and lacks
The stuff that makes horses happy or frisky,
Legumes and clover and such. They've only got
One goddamn gut, he says, not four like a cow.
Don't want 'em gettin' hay belly on empty calories…
Like what you been doin', he says, poking
My gut. Well, shit, why'd you wait so long
To cut my field, asshole, I say. He says,
When's the last time you fed it what comes out
The asshole, asshole—you know, cow shit, chicken
Shit, horse shit? Don't you know fields need it
To regenerate? I wish he weren't
So cantankerous on a tractor, so honest-
Abe about the chaff from the hay, or whatever.
His words scatter my thoughts like a tedder,
Toss them on horse shit and horse
Sense and hindgut of horse versus
The four-chambered stomach of cow. That's
What I'm chewing on now. Did I evolve
Like the horse, to be on the move, drift
Across grasses toward my next lean meal?
Or did I, somewhere along the way, turn
Domestic as a heavy-bellied sow or cow?
I sit down amidst the hayfields
And tally the lean years
From the fat… until my paunch overhangs
My pants. And now
It's late August, dust heavy on the leaves.
Young farmer's not even baling
The worthless stuff—just fluff,
He says, with no known nutrients.

HORSES STANDING IN RAIN

I love standing here
pelted by raindrops,
don't you? the old horse
woman says who has
trained Morgans most her
life and is so much
part of them she's outside
now in driving rain
shoveling their droppings
and smoothing the riding ring
as if it were clear weather.
Skin's so leathery
it's good rain
permeates the pores,
she says, and she loves
listening to trees clicking
in the wind, listening to raindrops
tick against fence posts,
to the slight hiss
of rain against electric
wires that keep her horses'
ears up. What's life
if not this, she says,
out in mud puddles
a child might splash through,
but she moves in her muck
boots with a full adult stride
then clicks her tongue
at the mares who nicker
back in their one and only
language of a rainy day.
(And yes, there are other
sounds for sunny days.)

LATE FALL

Nervous breakdown. Left the hoedown.
Left the hay bales, kale and Brussels
      Sprouts. Left the apples'

Frozen spoils, corvids coring them
With smart, sharp beaks, scattering
      Apple pulp to the brook trout.

Drove through the scarped Greens,
Body deep in the stuff of home, dry
      As bone, as granite. Drove away.

Spun roulette wheels beneath a chassis,
Swerved with city smarts, on the verge
      Of migraine, pain of

What's shed, what's housed, what's had.
Arrived with the verve of someone
      Auditioning Broadway

For a bit part in anonymity,
And dowsing for the downside of fortune
      Found a walk along the Hudson

Bracing. Found the stiff admixture
Of freshwater undercut by brackishness,
      Brash Atlantic overwriting

Every tributary with a local name,
Erasing any trace of home, replacing
      It with one vast abrasive.

UNDER THE RADAR

I'm so low on the priority list
I'm almost trackless.
I don't use stealth.
I don't scramble my signals.
I'm simply living off the grid,
mucking up the markets, gifting
whatever I make to anyone
with a private grudge against
business as usual. Is that life
enough? I like it here on the edge
of empire. The sun
seems to move from one
horizon to the other
where it rests and shines.
I'd like to move like that—
radiant and removed,
lit with an inner privacy
that sometimes hides
under a bushel,
sometimes shines
outward as a green
ray at sunset,
sometimes bursts
in auroras that
erase all Earth's
transmissions.

SPRING POEM, NYC

Five years in this city and I haven't written
A spring poem. I need to learn how to put
A passing cloud inside the steel and glass
Of a midtown high-rise; put a blooming
Tulip tree beside the downtown doorman
With his long-stemmed dustpan and brush scooping
Up fallen petals along with a dog's
Business on the sidewalk; put the man with
The leaf blower (hey buddy, it's just spring!)
Beside the house sparrow with its beak caught
In a grate; put car exhaust with the leaves
That will recycle it. My mind needs to bloom
New relations: the park raccoon and his
Country cousin, the dumpster seagull and his
Seacoast double. For every farmer's daughter
I celebrate in the hay, there's a woman in furs
Clacking down Broadway with 9-inch heels
Who is her own pedestal. Oh, what shall I do
with this city's profusion? Come to think
of it, spring's like that, the tulips abundant, unstable,
Unstoppable, cherry blossoms making me
Forget what I was thinking—I was thinking
The Hudson really is a magnificent
Ocean channeled all the way to Poughkeepsie!
All that sparkle and salt mixed with something
Smelling of bedrolls and clothes slept in for months.
I was thinking—all that piney solitude
I had in Vermont, traded for a city
Heavy on irony, denaturing Nature
As that old broad or god we haven't
The leisure or need or magical thinking
To long for—suddenly, over the horn honk
In gridlock, over sirens of fire and emergency,
Comes the obliterating rumble of thunder,
The cloudburst held in a fisted nimbus

From—of all places I thought I'd never
Utter—New Jersey, that land so fertile,
So full of spring, we loved it to death.

AND WHY NOT BE HAPPY

Not a question.   A lever you press
against the stone of your sorrow

to lift the world

as the grungy singer
on the subway platform

undoubtedly did

with her paisley pants and purple bandana
and beat-up fiddle scratching a few notes

that sent rats dashing toward the third rail

and rattling her black tambourine
with most of the metal discs missing

which served anyway as a measure
of the increments between

one brake-screeching train and the next,

and after the loudspeaker announced
the next one's approach,

she flashed her teeth and poured forth
a soprano so controlled so forceful

it could have come from nowhere other than
her decision to make it so

to make it a happiness

that lifted the day above itself
and opened the subway doors

and opened the listeners before we stepped over
the gap between platform and car

and rattled off into the dark.

EXILES

after Adam Zagajewski

And don't we all want a second life
in order to process the first one?

Don't we all want a second childhood
refunded at the end of days?

My mother said, You'll regret this for the rest of your life. I have.
My father said, Never too late to take over the business. It is.

My sister said, You betrayed me by running for the competition. I did.
My brother said, This trouble is partly your fault. It is.

My grandfather said, Wish I could live long enough to see what you become. He couldn't.
My grandmother said, Wish I could live long enough to see you heal. She did.

When I was a metaphysician, I roundly criticized my students
for writing about their families. And now, I'm almost out of ideas,
except this one: Write about family.

I eschewed elegies when I was young. Now, that's all I write—
letters to family and friends with no conceivable forwarding address.

And yet… the sun continues to blue the atmosphere and green the trees…
and will until the Milky Way collides with Andromeda in a pyrotechnics
best seen from a parallel universe.

And yet… the green snake continues to shock me in the garden…
if not the bellwether salamanders, fireflies, bobolinks.

And yet… life is as gorgeous and ravenous as it always was…
and still there is no consolation.

IN THE VILNIUS CAFÉ

In the famous Vilnius café,
where Miłosz once sat and scribed
his people's history, I sat in my sky-
blue shirt, partly obscured by a cloud-
white napkin, and peered down at a weathered
tablecloth, anchored by an electric
pink bowl of borscht flashing
back to the lighthouse on the Maine coast
I saw from the cottage porch long ago
where I sat long summers with my long-
gone grandmother, who came over from
the Old Country, this very Vilnius
that had stained the land red
with her kin, our collapsible
trays almost touching, her bowl
of borscht beside mine,
as she dipped the spoon in,
lifted it to her lips, and gave me
a sideways gaze, a stern invitation
to sip, delicately, deliberately,
the beet soup, as she was taught.

GOING FOR A DRIVE

I once judged it a failure:
Grandfather going for a drive
every morning of his retirement.
Dotage was the word that came to mind.
He was *in his dotage*. As if to say,
the wattage had gone out of the bulb.
The bright formulations had dimmed.
The word suggested endings. And care:
Some other must *do the doting*
on the dimming one. He drove the seacoast roads
and what did he see? The scintillant crests
and troughs of water, the brightly colored
lobster boats or bone-white sailboats scudding
across the channel? God knows…
With age, we know. Now I've reached his
august vantage, August morphing
to September, the bright orange
tractor in this morning's pasture, just
backing up to the tedder to spread the hay,
and twenty-seven turkeys scramble away
from where they'd been feeding off
the detritus of fallen grasses and wind-
fall apples, and the rotund farmer
in his bright blue overalls and red cap
waves his arms—almost affectionately?—
at them, as if to say, I'll see you for
Thanksgiving dinner. Now he waves
to me as I climb into the car for another
morning drive along the back roads,
where each day brings maple-changing
colors or the orange flash of a fox,
or the black dash of turkeys and more
turkeys crossing one pasture to another
as they feed and fatten for the fall.

DAD'S BEEN CRYING AGAIN

as if he were the valedictorian
of mourning. He's not a talker;
he taught us to be tight lipped
to pain. If we children cried,
he'd pinch our arms to teach us
there's always another hurt,
so just shut up. Dad's been crying again,
whose reservoir must be deep and long—
his 95 years of dammed streams
and rivers backed up and laid end
to end would reach from here to Mars.
That's the red planet, cratered, un-
stable, dusty with indifference,
masked with poisonous gas. Dad's been
crying again. He doesn't want to live
like the last astronaut in outer space,
but all his friends have gone
into the black vacuum before him
and he can't retain their names
or faces. His brain has made him shy
of something like a 3rd birthday, a time
before add & subtract & wash & dress
& make your bed. Unlike the kid
whose head will fill with facts and math
that lets him figure trajectories
of rocket ships, Dad's head
fills with one obliterating thought:
He'll soon be dead. He's crying again.
And who can blame him? And what for?
He's stored his tears for 90 years or more.
When not spanking a child, he wore a blinding
smile, a burly grace, a face unfazed by
ponderous circumstance. He aged and
aged, to an age where nothing's left
to chance but death. With brains so scrambled

he couldn't say if God invented man or man
invented Time. He couldn't say, for sure,
if cart preceded horse, the chicken the egg,
the universe its inverse. He can only say
for sure, he's forgotten how it ends but that
it ends. And then he cries again.

AFTER THE BLIZZARD

Sunlight stars a nub of icicle
growing from the gutter.

Beneath it, snowdrifts, wind-carved, canted like frigid
sailing ships, cantilevered over the deck,

deck chairs blasted, ragged canvas humped under snow,
and those that are overthrown, blown

clear off the deck, lie now under drifts like corpses.
Truth is, shapes shorn

of meaning could be conceived
as anything—windrows done with autumn, tomb-

stones in the family plot, buried under snow
so blown it's still frothing in the sun—as after

the heart stopped, the breath stopped, froth
was on her lip, glaze still on her eye, frosted as was her

permanent when the face shrunk into itself, and that curl, that wave
fluoresced under humming light above her,

and the gleaming apparatus of gurney with white sheets sailing
down the corridor, down a parting sea of orderlies

as the doors parted for one more charge of current against her chest
and after that, after the utter failure of white

to tremble again, rise again into drifts of consciousness,
eyes iced and shining a new lucidity, after that,

the white sheet closing over could have been a cart of dirty bedding
wheeled to laundry, could have been a snowdrift adrift,

could have been almost anything without meaning, except for
the one perceiving this nub of growth this morning,

this speck of gutter moisture that grows over the first,
as if forming a neck, a larynx, a new breathing apparatus,

a shiny new throat that lengthens in sun.

THE WASTING

He was deep in coma. He was warm
to my hand on his brow. Whatever furrows
the world's concerns had plowed into
his forehead were smoothed over now.

A bed lamp shone overhead. Now he was
inert as a sunlit stone, ready to merge
again with the earth. His breathing,
when it came, was even. No rasping

or panting. Someone said his breaths
were triggered not by the body's need
for oxygen, but by the buildup of
CO_2 in the lungs, our waste, needing

to be released into the world, and so,
the exhale, before the next inspiration.
Someone said, your dad is taking in
less from the world, no food, no water,

and so, less energy, less carbon, merges
with the body's oxygen, and less reason,
therefore, to exhale. Wasting away, we say,
wasting away, when there is no waste left

to promote the next breath. That was the stage
I found him in, or on, playing his part
in the final act. Someone had brushed his hair,
had placed a breathing tube beneath his nose.

Two hospice workers entered and said,
We're here to honor and to love your father.
Had I misheard the second infinitive?
They said it again: *to honor and to love.*

And thus began all my woe, as they placed
two pillows under his torso, gently
turned him first one way, then another,
to keep off the bedsores. Each time they re-

arranged his open mouth, which had crumbled
from the pull of gravity, until it was,
again, mostly a round O exposing
the speechless tongue, the shadows in his throat.

∞

Speak. Tell me of the blood rush and the blockage.
Tell me how the senses close: first the blackout
of the eyes, then the body's lost bearings
in the world, the tongue teeth-bitten as it

tries to describe the whirling vertigo,
the fire in the temples, the enormous
ache that comes from nowhere you can name.
Almost last, the scent of burnt fuses, smelling salts.

Speak. You can hear me. The last to go
are your ears. You can hear me saying no-
thing, struggling with that long suppression:
feeling. What do I have to say to you?

∞

I plant my hand on his forehead. *Caress it,*
I tell myself. I turn my hand over
and with the knuckle side, caress his brow.

Talk to him, I tell myself. No words come.
Say nothing, especially now, in his dying,
that is not true. Others would say otherwise:

Give comfort at all cost. My creed, such as
it is, is otherwise from their otherwise.
I will say nothing, or a few vague things:

*Well, here we are, at the end. You look calm.
I hope you're calm. I've flown through a storm
to be here. Can you hear me? I'm here now*

at the end. At your end. At the end.

∞

The doctor said, *Without food or water,
a failing body lasts at most a week.*
A hospice worker whispered, *I've known some*

to last for two. Someone on the night shift
swore the record was a month: *A body
lived without nutrition for a freaking month,*

he said, *a freaking month.* So much distance
in my gaze, I'm ashamed. We've never been
particularly close. That word, *particularly,*

the culprit. He'll die by degrees, my voice
said to my mind. My anger will leach, my love
will come, or, at least, I'll arrive at a neutral place.

As if perfect neutrality were peace.

∞

We sat another hour or two. I checked
his toes and fingers. Not blue. Not curling.
The doctor came to check his heart, his breath,

and feel his left leg. It's getting cold, he said.
And that means? It could be days, or hours. *Hours?*
It would be days, my voice said to my head.

I brushed my knuckles over his warm brow.
I listened for a minute to his five or
six breaths, I smoothed his hair, and then I left.

∞

That woe. Those Oreos stacked before him,
like Midas gold, gleaming in his eyes:
two piles, five-high, ready for devouring,
his just desserts for a day's work well done.

We are carbon creatures, our foods carbon,
our acids breaking it down, extracting it
from the body's deep mines, for energy.

So much, so much did he consume. The waste.
The want. The sugar, salt, and fat. The snack.
The snacking before meals. The meals.

The snacking after. The snacking between
TV ads, tubs of ice cream, bags of chips,
candy bars, cashew nuts, cans of Coca-Cola.

From dinner to bedtime, thousands of calories.
How does a man on a couch elevate
his respiration rate? How does a man inert
burn off the consequences of his waste?

∞

That woe. Because I could not love him.
Because unlike those hospice workers, who
knew him not, who honored him only

as generic man, because unlike them,
I who had lived with him had so much un-
resolved, so much deep, unacknowledged…
whatever it is that tears the world apart—
from him to me, from me to him—till death
us do part, so help me God I do have it.

∞

What was the ancient grudge between us?
That you banished my world, as I banished yours?

If poets are the unacknowledged
legislators, then legislate this: Traverse

the no-man's land between business
and verse, war and peace. Because you were

a foot soldier of the Second War and
I, a war resister. Because you could recall

all the war songs yet balk at the poetry
that shaped them, balk at that one word (of surrender),

poetry, province of the lily-livered, limp-wristed aesthetes…
now, near death, I will teach you its province and provenance.

Start with that sound you tartly called your art form:
It involves the mouth—as mine does—if not

the mind. You did this thing with your lips pulled
back, tongue pushing breath through your teeth, a quick

whistle, a word you made up, onomato-
poetic sound from your cheeks, a *sissle*,

grimacing like a gargoyle, a *sissle*,
whistling an old war tune, "Yankee Doodle."

This is my art, you said. *It rhymes with fart.*
That's your business, isn't it, big shot?

∞

Because unlike those hospice workers, who
knew him not, I had lived under his roof,
had broken his bread, had owed him all,
then nil, had played the prodigal, had not
returned, or had returned only in body—
Just spend time with him, Mother said, *just sit*
beside him on the couch and watch TV
together and have a snack—had struck
tennis balls back and forth across a net;
had struck golf balls together toward a distant green;
had struck up one faltering conversation after another—
because what I loved was nothing to him, nothing.

∞

That TV show from which he quotes:
Yabadabadoo! That's Fred Flintstone, actor
closest in looks and actions to my father.
And he's a fucking cartoon character!

Yabadabadoo's not rocket science.
Not $E=MC^2$, not *Cogito ergo sum*.
It's paralingual sound, that is, sound
streaming alongside language, without

the smart referentiality. It's
pragmatic, expressive as an upraised
club swung around a yawping caveman's head.
Yabadabadoo! Yabadabadoo!

Which could mean, *I feel great!* or *Go cook me*
a flaming brontosaurus steak, and I'll

feel even greater! It sounds like a noogie
to the noggin. Like a happy wedgie. Like

a victory lap after Flintstone's feet
have raced the caveman car around the track.
It sounds like Archie Bunker's *Edith!* or
Ralph Kramden's *One of these days, Alice—pow!*

Straight to the moon! but with less meaning
and less aggression. It's an exultant
sound—*Happy as a pig in shit*—my father's
other Top 10 Hit in the annals of analogues.

And now he lies all out of words
or paralingual meaning, just the steady
six breaths in a minute, each one heavy
as a stone at the caveman quarry.

∞

A call from hospice: 2:00 a.m. The night
nurse reports my father's done with sleep,

with breath, the brief ritual of details:
diuretics as his lungs filled with fluid,

morphine as panic and terminal pain
seized the body. And then he slipped away.

∞

I said I wouldn't, damn it. No metaphors.
But God, when the chapel director
shows us a side door, we enter and see

the body laid out in a cardboard box,
as we'd agreed, the body in its hospice
gown, as we'd agreed, the body slightly

bloodied at the breastbone from where they plucked
the pacemaker, a slight shock, and more shocking,
the body's face made up to look like—no,

this simile, this counterfeit, was not
my doing, I who long ago despised
the mortician's deceitful hand—this face,

this old-man's face looks like a youthful
father, facsimile of someone I'd known
in boyhood when he lifted me skyward—

but no—being in cold storage for three days,
his face, when I touch it, is, as the dead
metaphor goes, cold as stone.

∞

Rest In Peace. Why is the acronym
an antonym: RIP? Where he is: peace.
Where I am: torn. Broken piece of the world.
And, therefore, shorn of peace. He's cremated,

his body gone to ash, his wholeness
delivered out of whole cloth to an urn.
Ridiculous. Why purge and burn the corpse
if not to cast him broadside by a generous

hand? Not one of us is so generous.
My mother wants his ash if not his essence
sealed in an urn sealed in a mausoleum
beside her own corruptible body.

Did he wish some dollop of him had been
scattered into mountain wind or sea breeze
or gusts along a golf course? No one knows.
His living will and last testament are

silent on the matter of scattering
matter to the four winds or windless tomb.
What's the answer to the riddle of a man
with no last wishes? To follow mindlessly.

∞

Rest in peace, father. That faker in the cardboard box
is not you, nor is that cheated ash and dust in the urn.
Rest in peace, our memories remain the only vessel
worth mattering, worth holding your matter, father.

Conflicted, conflated, shrunk, or smooth as death on your brow,
these memories are all we have of you now; they're ours until
they pass with us, or pass out of our minds, into timelessness.
They are what we know as love for a father, a stranger,

who brought us here to matter, and to the brink of matter.
Rest in peace, father. You have carried our terror farther
than you could know, simply by being father, carrying
our fears a while in the world, carrying us out of many

dark places, carrying us now to the edge where your own
small matter expands into the gathering immensity

∞

Now you're gone and that mouthed *sissle* sounds
in my head its untranslatable

intimacy. It is sound beyond sense,
though not senseless—echo of who you were.

That *sissle* and those round Oreos you
once consumed are now consumed in my mouth

after the memorial service, sweet
chocolate and cream wafers linking time

to timelessness. And the sound that swells
triumphant from your throat long after

your breath is stopped is *Yabadabadoo!*
as meaningless as it is enduring.

II

SEAGULL IN A BOWL

I can hear the seagull in a bowl
As I scrape with a metal spoon the last yogurt
From the rim—*scraw, scraw, scraw, scraw*—
And hear the ocean the undertow the wash
Of wave and wind holding the bird aloft.
There's a slight metallic ringing in the sea
As if the boats and buoys and harbor bells
Swamped from a winter storm or rogue wave
Still clang beneath the blue. And the dream
I had before breakfast of white goats, bells
Tinkling lightly under their beards, high up
In a Greek harbor town, milked and pastured
Where the bees make their amber combs
And the serving girl comes with her morning figs
Yogurt and honey to set on the wooden table
Already warm with sun and blue cornflowers,
Her black hair brushing my shoulder as she bends…
Or that other height from the amusement park pier,
Where gulls scavenge and float above the arcade,
Where waves break against the risings and pilings,
And the ring-toss winner sets off the dinging bell
And the girl laughs as the boy hands her a souvenir
And she spoons frozen yogurt into his soft mouth…
I can hear all of it as my metal spoon scrapes
The rim of the bowl where memories circle and rise
To my mind and mouth like a first lost kiss.

RODIN'S *LE BAISER*

It must feel wonderful—
full of wonder—to kiss
like that, forever, sealed
to each other and to
your maker if Rodin's
the god designing your
lips the muscles of which
pull the cheeks to pucker
and suck, gently—for this
will be forever—suck
the lips' flesh, tongue's juices,
lover's breath, pledge unsaid,
the lovely mons Venus
the pulsing Mandrake root,
all forces gathered *here*,
precisely, where the god's
hands molded all that is
constant and inconstant
to a bronzed point where
covenants are made and
broken as two bodies
come together and pull
apart, but *here*, here is
their perpetual pact,
her head cupped under his
uplifting palm as if
quaffing a potion, her
arms curled upward guiding
his head gently, keenly,
down toward hers, the moment
of their concentration
total on this place which—
temple, sanctum, altar—
will be forever sealed
with the bronze from a god's
jealous, blessing fingers.

CEZANNE'S ATELIER

                              Aix-en-Provence, France

Cezanne this. Cezanne that. Rue Cezanne's
the rue Cezanne mounted every day
he could for his coveted view: Mont

Sainte Victoire. 60 times! 60 times
he washed his canvas in rabbit-skin
glue, lime dust, titanium white.

He sanded, gessoed, spread the oils,
built shapes so geometrically precise...
There must not be a single loose strand,

60 times (60!) Cezanne was Cezanne,
the same, yet not the same, as color,
line, form transformed the mood of Sainte

Victoire. The artist's brush and mind made
landscape sit up or lie down, beget
or withhold, surrender or conquer.

Cezanne's atelier, sandstone ochre,
red shuttered, with a missing fourth wall...
a single gap through which the tension,

almost theatrical, all windows,
facing north for natural light—almost
unnatural to let a model, a

nude, into this bethel of blue sky—
his love was a mountain that taught him
to paint, to be, first, faithful to shape,

its natural features, and then, over
years, to blur what it was, as if first...
the light, the truth can escape... The eye

love were love, then never enough, must
be viewed in many moods, rouged, smoothed,
roughened, deepened with panels of blue

and green, orange and brown, heightened with
pigments from oil brush or palette knife.
Above all, given its true perspective,

time on time, as the vision within
took over and that lovely Sainte Victoire...
is not enough; it needs to think as well.

GREAT CITIES

One goes to the great cities of the world

partly to enter the past

through the portals and porticos of museums

Then the present frippery—

whatever one names the cycles

of ostentation and obsolescence—

has a sobering context

from Uruk to Ashur

to Sumer to Nineveh

and as always

all falls away—

some wise one says

who is now dust—

The gods gave us death

and kept for themselves life—

and so

leave the clay tablets with cuneiform

orders for goblets and idols

and go out into the city

to quaff your cup

THE BAND'S VISIT

after the Broadway show

The art of growing old resides inside
the imagery, she seemed to say, jasmine
wind, honey in the ear, spice in the mouth,

phrases this Israeli sang in her desert-
parched, dark-haired longing for some
Omar Sharif to float in from an oasis

mirage. Now an Egyptian commander
sat before her, a conductor conducting
her to hear through his dreaming fingers

strains of a minor-key melody swirling
out of his strict and loveless past, a desert
regret that might still be watered this side

of paradise, if only the music's bridge
could hold. Could it hold? No. For he could not
shed the weight of his seven skins of remorse,

his child's suicide, wife's wasting away,
and now all that remained was this abstraction,
loss, heavy with duty, for which he could not

conjure a sigh or tear, something that would dry
or dissipate. No, just this strict forbearance,
this stiff martial watch over the site of sacrifice.

She sighed and waved a restless hand. Maybe
the bridge *should* crumble, for this was not
paradise, just a wished affair, a comfort for two

loveless ones, and the minor key of that music begged
for melancholy drenched in wetness that touches
the earth and delivers jasmine sadness, the promised

fig and honey, the kofta and koshary, baklava and umm ali—
no, just distant memories as she beheld this curiosity,
this desert visitor, who had stirred her

so the bitter fed the sweet, the skin beginning
to crust and sag exuded a brilliant suppleness,
songs of Umm Kulthum perfumed the air

before fading to desert static, and the aphrodisiac hint
of coriander and cumin in the wind brought moisture
from the great river and the great sea beyond where

everything surges on its surface and then falls back.

WAVES GOING OUT, WAVES COMING IN,

    swells of seaweed, plant wanderers, wave drifters,
burlap sacks, ropes of polypropylene, one beat-up duck boot—all

        made of language—scraps of mollusks, flints of calcium carbonate

poking up from beach sand—abraded quartz and limestone—or from hard silt ridges
below tideline revealing green sea glass, an old Moxie bottle top and

someone's spent prophylactic, showing how the spawn
generates, eventually, from inland seas, dumping am-

phibians upon a landmass green with a new phylum a new order to take dominion

and the body straightway changes color, chameleon, and form, rock
clasper, tree climber, two-footer, evolver

into this morning's clots of fog where shell collectors seem to float in and out

      of existence, scumbled, then daubed in pink bikinis or blue swimsuits,

bent over green plastic shovels, unearthing from the bubbling

    mudflats the clams that will open

        in tonight's pit of seaweed and fire

and surrender their soft anatomies, almost human—

     mouth and gut, heart and nerve, intestine, anus,
labial palps (those first antecedents of lips and language) and one powerful

burrowing foot (tunneling away)—surrender

    to the grasper's opposable thumbs, the sucker's bilabial lips.

MATING BEHAVIORS OF STORKS, EGRETS, HUMANS

We're out of love again and wandering
with other birdwatchers over the cedar shakes,
spying on spring nesting sites where great
migrations end and settle into familiar patterns

of rearing and weaning. We're here
not so much to learn or unlearn
lessons we don't already know but simply
to lose ourselves in observation, in strange

cries and croaks and wattle rattles, in the dusting
of wings with swamp wind, leaves, thistle.
Half of me watches the nesting dance and joust
of wood storks and egrets, while half my mind

flits to the Ukraine-Russian war half a world away,
the "mindless slaughter," as newsmen say,
when really, it's horribly mindful, murderous intent,
artillery flattening the homes of millions,

the old shashka slicing a path to the Black
Sea. It's a human thing that separates me from the wild
life I'm here to see. I see wood storks all concentration
on the moment of their perpetuating. Clattering bills

clipping the feather fluff of their mates' necks,
perhaps part of the ritual of their coupling.
I've not spoken a kind word all morning
to the one I've mated with for life. Nor has she

turned toward me. Or away from me. Like many of us,
she maintains a studied neutrality, a learned distance.
Why are we here? To walk the boardwalk's circuit,
cedar shakes buoying us over the swampy spaces,

letting us bridge the distance between these fleshly beings with calculating hearts and minds and those winged creatures lost in the present moment of their mating, almost oblivious of us.

LOCAL FREEZE

Delray, Florida, March 13, 2022

Northerner, stranger, I've been visiting my failing mother in her gated
golf community. Yesterday, I wandered under the gumbo limbos,
thinking of her inevitable descent, while green iguanas scattered
under the fallen copper succulents. Flat lines of black clouds
rolled over the Everglades, pelting the land with cold rain,
then, briefly, almost impossibly, hail, over the wetlands and dredged
fields, reminding us how fragile the grapefruits and oranges.
Indoors, the TV's evening broadcast was almost unbearable,
tank columns crushing the suburbs as they advanced on Kyiv,
so at dawn, it's almost unsurprising to hear herons scream
outside in the bluing jet stream and something hump and gurgle
under the roofline, roosts of ibises, perhaps, unsettled by this sudden
cold snap from the north and mass murder half a world away
lit on everyone's CNN flat screen with their morning coffee,
bulldozers plowing bodies into mass graves and the newscaster's
dim analysis numbing us despite the caffeine hit.

I slip on a coat and slip out to the screened porch, watching small lizards
the color of cement stiff on sidewalks, stuck to their pre-dawn spots
until sun and body temps rise, but now they're sitting ducks
for electric lawn carts, a few workers rattling by with rakes and shears.
Beneath their wheels, the sod's tough enough to harbor earthworms
still aerating the soil, and lower down, layers of helium push upward
like optimism, bolstering the earth's crust where a cold line of ants,
stunned and listless, makes no advance from pizza crust to ant nest.
If I lift my head and look back through glass doors to the living room,
I can see the flat screen, those columns of tanks stuck outside Kyiv,
their husks burnt from stinger jets and drone strikes, punished
for scorching the earth earlier elsewhere where everything on,
and under, it, either perished or surrendered, and nevertheless,
perished. From here I can click the remote, shift to a local channel
where the morning forecaster hasn't yet decided whether we'll dodge
the freeze or whether all the fruit will perish.

QUESTIONS FOR A CORMORANT

Ossabaw Island, Georgia

Is this our oldest pact, cormorant, both sunning
on rotting wood, you on an old piling,
me on a ruined dock? We're both drawing warmth
from an old source that's still winding down.
Nearby, cranes yank machinery off oily tugs
to repair the hurricane-ravaged bridge, update
the washed-out road, restore the battered villa.
We won't live to see it finished, I guess,
but that's the way of progress, cormorant.
Wind moves the waves and the day moves along.
Utter stillness scares me… for the obvious
reasons. Don't mistake me, I'm glad to be here,
retired, loitering through hours of sun.
How else to savor? What do your senses
sense today, old cormorant, and why do I
imagine you old? Perhaps it's the fish hook snagged
in your yellow bill, a bloodshot look to your red eye.
How's the next poem to begin, build, and end?
Tell me, cormorant. Will it contain this sun?

CORMORANTS IN FULL SUN

Ossabaw Island, Georgia, 2018

Corruption in Congress was getting to me.
Never mind the White House. Perspective
was what I needed. I walked to the dock
in noon light, a clutch of cormorants
perched on wood pilings, a black mass
of outstretched wings reaching for the sun.
Killdeer cries in the mudflats. Red-billed
oystercatchers skimming over the sanctuary.
Tripling the military budget? For what?
They were already in Russia's back pocket!
The cormorants looked nonplussed. They didn't
care about some orange-haired, orange-skinned
nutjob who was going to obliterate their world,
and mine. They knew the moment was sweet,
even if they wouldn't say it, but sun on black
wings looked so soothing I said it
for them. I wanted to know only what
they knew, this moment… tide ebb exposing
the slick mud of the river emptying
into this brackish channel. Salt stung
my eyes. The salt marsh showed strange
incongruities, mud lumps, hollows, holes
bubbling with covert life, sea lice, water
bugs scriggling along the surface, the feel
of it, somehow, shaky, too much I couldn't
track or interpret. The cormorants took it all in,
or didn't, impossible to know what
their red eyes, craning on snaky radar
necks, recorded. I recorded only what
my senses sensed, what made sense
as a coherent set of intel. Old Roger
came puttering round the cove in his fishing
rig, a few old boys with him, MAGA caps

clamped to their heads. As they bumped
against the dock, I saw honey-colored bottles
of Maker's Mark, that whiskey going down
as smooth at noon as cocktail hour. The cormorants
stirred a little, ruffling their wings, in salute,
perhaps, or recognition. Were they all in it
together? When the old boys raised their tumblers
of glowing amber to the sky, I wasn't sure
it was for me, the birds, or their leader.
I gave a weak wave and watched the waves
beyond their boat that seemed, under this strong sun,
not waves at all but three-paneled triangles
colluding to wash over this undefinable,
moving thing we'd all agreed to call water
and the wavering moment. Enough to trick
us into thinking the world was solidly
what it was, and waves were waves, not
momentary shapes shifting at the whim
of whoever was in charge of perceiving.
One moment, wind made the waves move and the day
move along. The next, when wind stilled
and cormorants' black wings lost their luster,
the individual feathers appeared more
like black daggers, and the stillness
at the center of the day terrified.

BIG WINDS

Johnson, Vermont, July 2016

Big winds in the back pasture this morning.
Must have blown in from that dark bluster
in Ohio where the orange-haired dystopian
shouted himself red: a nation broken
and only himself with enough narcissistic
moxie to fix it. What would he fix? Short,
as always, on specifics. But the fix, so
far, fixates on anyone who crosses him.
In short, big winds blow from the small
mind of a bully who charges every flagging
patch of red. And half the nation's ready
to blow in his blowhard direction.
They're small children who want
a power daddy to fix what's broke.
And the big winds in the back pasture
presage afternoon thunderstorms and
a dome of hot air crushing down on us
that feels like the beginning of intolerable
conditions. A whole summer and autumn
of unbearable heat, which will roast the air
to record highs. If there's a weather god
today, he's a strongman. All those grass heads
below are dried out, hollow, blown in one
direction: his. The one turkey wading
through them is the steadiest creature in the field,
flattening the unthinking reeds, feeding as it needs,
and popping out onto lawn, finally, like a reality
TV star to shake off its crown of fluff and seed,
and now I see he's no turkey, he's a red-faced turkey
vulture, perfect for the cleanup work to come.

SO WHAT

So what if I've been lying to myself
about the oil wells and solar panels,
the fracking lease and hybrid cars?
So what if energy comes from Starbucks
lattes I scarf down before workouts
at the Fitness Club, and after the sweat,
I kill off a murder of beers at the pub.
So what if my former life forgets me
and all the hiking trails of my youth
lead to a treadmill and a universal
set of weights where what doesn't
crush you makes you stronger.
So what if all the crows have flown
from the forest perch beside my home.
The oil checks keep coming
from old Indian grounds, and I knock down
another brace of beers as I dream of solar
flares captured in kilowatts on my roof.
Everything's converted, finally, to energy
or money, or its opposite, flabby inefficiency.
So what if I can't tell the difference.
With a flip of the switch, I can cue up
the kind of blue on a stereo that once
made me cry and feel righteous.
Nod at an old love song, its scratchy refrain—
*saggy bed, soggy bottom, Bo Diddley lost his
hard-on, and I don't care.* My response to the past
is *whatever.* Now, even Miles' cool blue shoulder
shrug, *So What*, doesn't dent my consciousness,
doesn't change the tempo of my emotional ticker.
Even turned up loud, until the house groans,
So What doesn't make me behave better
than the worst sonufabitch, the best Samaritan.
Doesn't send me outdoors to shoot the crows
or shoo them off to sail in morning armadas
scavenging the day's ordinary treasures.

PEACOCKS, FOR EVANS

> "The Peacocks," from Bill Evans' posthumous
> album, *You Must Believe in Spring*

The tune was modal, ghosted,
like every tune since LaFaro
crashed in '61, melodic,
but he blocked it with stacked
fourths, plus some Asian thing
he'd brought back from the
Tokyo tour, sort of cupped
his fingers and clapped a
chord, like sad applause he'd
heard in Oslo. His first wife
Elaine gone under a train.
Then he shot a line
from mid-register to
upper and thought of the
junk and needle in his studio
drawer. Powdered a right hand
that rung the out-of-tune
upper octaves until a piano
tuner somewhere hung
his head. And soon, brother
Harry's undoing. Bill relaxed
into a liminal mood,
on the way to a place
of pure duration. So much
time between the voicings
of a ballad—time to find
a gone sister, a brother or two—
five-finger slides with the right
hand, chromatic overtones,
double-octave runs, odd
pentads he'd perfected
in Japan when the junk
really took. His hair looked

wild. His graying beard
became him. Still, the hunched
posture, the holy head bowed
to the piano. Dark glasses led him
further in. Arpeggios, twinned
an octave apart, echoes
in the canyons of the strings—that clarity
of feeling, giving the ghost
of the root, nothing more—a fading
bass line plucked from the earth,
musical notes hanging in the road-
side trees. Look in vain
for a through line. He's not
mainlining it. Instead, he's looking
for shaped figures in his solos, conjured
ghosts, gone-ness made manifest—
modal, tonal, total. Miles said, early on,
*The sound he got was like crystal notes,
sparkling water cascading from a clear
waterfall.* By the end, it was vapor,
trails dissolving in Manhattan sky.

THAT SAD CLAPPING

after the horn goes silent—
applause that crushes the way the singer comes back
into the song—something undeniably sad
about those clapping hands, historical, pressed into the grooves
of "Body and Soul"
as permanent as the singer's voice
or the bruised trumpet, coaxing something
from her—some ache she didn't know
was hers—and she was
answering… before the sad
clapping cut her off—something
almost mindless about that clapping,
obligatory, as if
paying the cover charge, the bar tab,
not at the center of things
but trying to grease the wheel,
etch the groove,
so it'll spin out another day's
blandishments before time
goes dark. But *she* knows
time as well as God does, knows
it because she's human, knows
how to measure it—how to
parse it and hold it
and parcel it out, and God's
demoted to the swish
of the drummer's brushes
against skins. God's no longer
even a slurred order
for another round
of effervescence, or something
fiery, light on the water.
No, he's just a brace
in the song's bridge,
where the horn comes in

and bends the tune almost
to breaking, then doesn't,
leaving it for the singer to do—
and those sad hands clap right through
it, as if they didn't know
it was a bridge to the far
side of what makes
feeling felt, as if
they hadn't heard the call
and response—or as God
might say, the annunciation
and ascension—and really,
for most of them, it does
passeth understanding,
doesn't it? And isn't that
exactly the point?
They're glad there's a blessed
thing in this world
that says it for them,
that plumbs time for them,
that plucks up a millionth of the mystery,
rolls it around the bones, the throat,
and eases it out, into the world—
to which the name "Body and Soul"
has been given. And even if
they can't quite name it,
maybe that's enough.

LIKE BLUE BEHIND A DAYTIME MOON

> "Life teaches you really how to live it, if you live long enough."
> —Tony Bennett, commenting on Amy Winehouse's death,
> four months after their duet recording of "Body and Soul"

Some of us are born with death in our voice.
It comes bawling out of us, colicky baby, rattling
The voice box, and do what we will—drug it, drown it

In drink, smother it in song—we hear it stutter, syncopate,
String against pattern a hesitation
So profound, pronounced—it triumphs, Amy,

Because of the way your voice keeps bending a word, a phrase,
Until it molders, immaterial, and behind the solid word
The void shows through, like blue behind a daytime moon.

It comes right through the staves, the measures, the chords
Built from a solid root, piled upward on a stem promising
An imagined harmony, lyrics promising a story

That adds up—all of it de-composed by death—and it's not
As if we run screaming from it. No, we desire it, hoard it,
Award it golden trophies, with your voice, Amy,

As its messenger. Death blows right through the notes,
Rips the words apart, into their im-
Material sounds, bends them, pliable, permeable, until

They're unrecognizable, ciphers signaling only the stink
Of endings, charnel house full of wine, poison
Of liver, shutdown of heart and brain, blackout

From which you shall not awaken, a final white sheet thrown over
The immodesty of it all. "I just sing. Just let me sing.
That's all I can do," you say, days from your end—

Death's voice breathing through the booze, the drug haze,
Your voice spliced with lines so pure, so white, nothing
Whole or individual could possibly survive; no, it's all just smashed

Together into so much bright or dark matter and extruded through
          wherever
The chasm-hum of the beginning-of-the-end is—and maybe death is
Just the immensity within us, Amy, always trying to express itself.

HOW SHE GOT THAT VOICE

after Dorianne Laux

Take a voice like that: a 4-minute poem pressed
at 45 rpm, a voice that hugs to some center
of gravity solid as a cylinder, and even though
we can't know it, we know there's more, something scratched
on the flip side just ready to burn us, and now
take that voice down to its native range, say, to 33 rpm,
spin it slow, slower, letting the voice sink deeper in each groove,
and lower the pitch, until it might be the most haunted thing
you've ever heard about a mother's lingerie, a father's fifth
of whiskey, a drugged brother, a drowned sister,
and let that voice confess if she had it to do again, if
God offered to raise that pitch to a grating 78 of comedy
and she could cruise through life with a helium laugh, she'd
still ditch that clan deep in its own shit and circumstance,
still hitch herself to the first car headed on a road trip out of there,
and even as she drove off feeling her voice unspooling, rising
to meet the road's momentum, she'd begin to feel a backward pull, umbilical,
strong as tempered steel coiled to her own bumper, slowing her down, slower,
slower, until two momentums, pulling in different directions, reached a still point,
and she drove forward as her favorite writers had always promised, forward
into the past, and what had started as a high-pitched peal of release
now caught in the misfire of cylinders, the car straining as if hauling
a trailer filled with junk belongings, the grind of metal on metal making
a burr and growl on some part of the engine block, the eventual oil leak
that would drain her, take her down to a slow burn and make her voice
      her voice.

THERE IS NO SADNESS

after reading James Wright: A Life in Poetry

There is no sadness like today's sadness—
a spring day so achingly alive I want to break
out of my body. But somebody already said that.
I want to join the host of dandelions on the lawn.
Somebody almost said that, too. Are we nothing
but reproductions? I want to join the fledgling
leaves on the maples, the last straggling catkins
on the birch limbs, the ravens rubbing their
three toes in the sun-warm garden, the green
beetles hauling pebbles over bluestone.
Enough already with description, some surly
yenta yells from a lower East Side tenement
window in my head. She doesn't know a seed
from a shiksa from a sonnet but she claims
some part of me, too. I think she uses the same
nest as phoebes under the eaves that shit
on my crime lights, necessary or unnecessary
because the nearest neighbors are miles off.
Minus a shotgun, a crime light does the trick,
pushing back the margins of the ominous. And now,
fear has crept in over the dandelions and ravens.
My eyes are filled with light this morning and still
darkness crowds the edges where rods conquer
cones. Or is it the other way? Knowledge dogs
us, turns us out of the garden, over the biting-
fly pastures, and into the ticked-infested woods.
And on into the world where generations begat
and beget and there is no ending, is there, except
for something upending as elegy in which
we inherit no sadness like today's sadness.

FINIFUGAL

Finifugal: shunning the end of anything.
Yes, there's a word for what makes us human.
When we gaze in the mirror, we approve ourselves
six nanoseconds ago, the time light requires to bounce
from the glass's dark underside to our eyes. *I see black
light*, said Victor Hugo, dying. And every evening,
we *advesperate*. The sun's guillotined from the sky,
and we think of the *tricoteuse* in France, knitting, un-
knitting as the heads rolled. We think of the old *apricity*,
the warmth of sun in winter. And some of us miss the full light
of language, the archaic and the obsolete. What if we used
its full lexical range? All twenty volumes of the *OED*,
130 pounds, 59 million words. What if we had time
for the research? Would it matter if we knew
"that girl is hot" because fornicate comes from *fornus*,
an oven, a furnace? Would that put people off? Would it hurt
to know Earth's magma will, finally, blast *pyroclasts*
in trails of broken fire when it's hot enough, or worse, to know
Earth's flirting with the moon, its fickle push and pull,
impels her from us a few millimeters more each year,
and the planet slows its rotation one nanominute. In the time
of hot-blooded dinosaurs, each day clocked twenty-three hours.
Does that give people pause? Does it matter the meter's ticking faster?
That meter and measure are one; meter and moon and menses
are one; meter and month and meal do the same work, measuring time?
And we're back to shunning the end of anything: *finifugal*.

III

LINES WRITTEN AT TYRONE GUTHRIE

Tyrone Guthrie Arts Center, Ireland

I've seen one drifting on the lake
Alone—an old cob muddling
By the desiccated nest among the rushes.
Now there's no rush; the pen's gone,
The cygnets flown; he'll not mate again.
His wings fold down; he rarely flies;
He seems to let the currents take him

Where they will. And this was once
A bully swan that with a single wing
Could brush a yapping dog back
On its head, or when a swimming man
Approached the nest, the swan rose up
And dive-bombed him until he flailed
And sputtered and was drowned.

The fight in him is over now.
He's purposeless as water.
Retired, he's earned a steady diet
Of watery roots and tubers…
Until his bill's serrations
Finally fail or a fox takes him
In his dotage as if he were a quail.

LINES WRITTEN AT TYRONE GUTHRIE

Another day of slant rain
that comes in sheets and obliterates
the landscape for minutes of time
and yet there are spaces between

through which one can almost see
a body or two, tucked in, refusing day's
advance, coiled under a comforter,
like delayed half-rhymes

in a love duet—sweet banter
before the dead reckoning,
the friar delivering his liquor
that yields *the likeness of shrunk death*

for two-and-forty hours, from which
like a sprung rhythm the youthful
one will spring up again…
if only. The day is like a Guthrie

production that wants to be high
art but can't quite kick-start itself
out of malaise, so it kicks around the manse,
waiting for funding and the producer's say-so—

he thinks it'd play better as an off-Broadway
show, risqué, that's just made its way
uptown to where the lay crowd hangs
out, and keeps its clothes on—but never mind.

The rain's washed over the lake and hills and
away it goes. The lake and hills remain.
I'll need to send the lady away, buckle
my buckle, and buckle down, refrain

from playing with language and other
things just for thrills, or frills, and
grill myself or my environment
with the sorts of questions

that lead to an intent, as intent
appears to lead to meaning,
and meaning to meat, and meat's
the matter, and matter's an end.

LINES WRITTEN AT TYRONE GUTHRIE

The wind is up: It wipes that placid look right off the face
Of the lake and turns to frowns and wrinkles all content.
Times like this, I'm bent on fame, embarrassed as I am
To say it, and all my equanimity goes slack or turns
To grimaces as the wind comes up: The last flowering
Trees are blown to hell. A bell in the wind signals the start
Of the hellhound race. My mind makes them lap the track
And howl when only one can win: The rest conspire to eat him.

One angry down draft: Ripples start on the far shore and fan out
In vectors violent as a temper tantrum or a Chinese fan
On whose face one reads a hundred years' war: cherry blossoms
Scattered onto blood trails; a flock of storks disordered in the air,
Buffeted upside and down, tumbling under boot heels
Of the marching army. Oh, how my mind makes a mess
Of something simple as a springtime gale! You'd think
That reputations were for sale, and not earned the hard way:

Word by word. There is no grace. The wind hurries the clouds
Along at a pace too fast for thunder or the lightning strike.
They're just wild, like leaderless, spooked stallions or grey-
Hounds who've lost the track, the comfortable oval upon
Which their brilliant speed begins to look like art, like smart
Intention, and not some useless burst of energy that blows
The whole pack in a frightful, confused tumble off a cliff,
The wind whirling in their anxious, dying ears: *if, if, if, if.*

This morning's world is wild with wind: If we're not rooted deep
And stiff with resistance, like trees surviving by the shore,
We're blown to hell and back before we know it. To bend
Is also useful, and to bow, and to let the wind blow itself
Out through the shaded spaces between our ribs where a clinging
Nest might be. Let the wind blow away, let it bundle its violence,
With no mind at the reins, let it blow over hills and down to the sea.

LINES WRITTEN AT TYRONE GUTHRIE

One more sunny day in which there are no answers.
The lawn man comes to trim the grass, as if it mattered.
The Irish bluebells, thick along the path, teach green
a blue thing or two for a quick week before they pass.
Are they happy, sad? Do they care? Am I asking
the right proprietors? Let's take the largest lens
we've got, place it on the sky and look back to the Big
Bang's near-beginning, a mere million years from the Original
Nothing, when out of the blackest chasm came gases
that with a scratch and match burst into suns and solar flares—
and tell me if, in that first fueled springtime, there's matter
that matters. No, I'm not just nattering on, though yes,
I am, I'm doing what we do in the midst of twiddling
thumbs in a void, I'm voiding myself of expectations,
of heavenly vacations, of hell's glam-hot coastline,
and I'm going to take my goddamn time with a chaise longue,
dragging it out on the new-clipped lawn to lie in nothing
but uncertainty, not a day more, just today's alluring
sunny skies under which I'll wish and wish for rain.

LINES WRITTEN AT TYRONE GUTHRIE

Two hours rambling over gorse-studded pasture. I'm hoarse
from shouting yellow yellower than the sun and more vanilla
than aether! Even the swans honk their approval of my out-
and-about and general brightening of the disposition. In this
country where every second shadow's attached to a sinner,
they drink to excess but follow the hedgerows and stumble home
for dinner. Agnostic as I am, I haven't talked to God
along a nature trail, nor met a god I ever liked that wasn't
in a lotus posture: not Buddha—for I'm fond of women
and prefer Guanyin meditating amidst the marsh marigolds
or Mary, cross-legged, sniffing roses in a topiary manger,
or someone out of time like Gaia-Tellus who I believe
as I believe the Earth is round and spinning on a phallus.
I'm lost. We're lost. God cast us out when Modernists
miscast him or wished him dead. And he's been dead
ever since, or turned his back on us, a black monolith
in space the greatest telescope can't penetrate. We've lost
the light from that old signal that goes back before the Big
Bang. That's why our postmodernists obsess for signs
of icy H_2O in distant universes and track back
now almost to the blast of the first Big Whimper, perhaps
just a temper tantrum God'd thrown from another unbelieving
swarm of stars and planets, our parallel, our oldest lesson before
our sun was warm. Hell, what can I know beyond the mute
swan's honk who, if his name were true, would be original
as silence, or sin, or sun, though I'm told there's a hiss and hum
from the gases. We're perfect asses here on Earth. What's it worth
to know that gods are gone, ghosts are phony, the fore-known
and the after-known are ignorant of us and us of them? It's worth
my life, I guess, my sixty years vexed by the cradle that rocked me
from my first foundations, to my earnest vernal search, to my selva
oscura in the dark woods of middle life, to this very moment
growing always closer to the age of God who is ageless, unless
I clap my hands and scare off the swans and sing for all I'm worth,
though it be nothing, a yellow stain and sting along the hedgerow home.

LINES WRITTEN AT TYRONE GUTHRIE

Gray weather—a little salt-and-pepper in the beard
Of this sky but don't say it out loud because a faux
Sun, pasted on, thinks it's still shining, though really,
Just in fits and starts, as clouds mass and billow by.
It's the old story, told again, how 6-foot-6 Tyrone,
65 to a day, still sleek in form, to celebrate,
Swam the whole damn lake. They told this story
At his wake. And how his wife, Lady Guthrie, flustered
In her late fifties, appeared in the dining room one night,
Her New York guests fresh from shopping sprees at Macy's
In their elegant threads, but Lady Guthrie came down dressed
For bed, a ratty gown she wore "around the house," as she said,
Though the house was a manse that might have asked for
Evening gowns, but no one frowned at her 6-foot frame
Entering the room (*like a sleek tree wrapped in moss*).
She dined with all the rest and made the most brilliant
Conversation. I have it on the word of an Irish actress
Who attended her cremation. These stories shine
From the fabled past as if they could push the dying
Gloom away and show us how to live with gray. Gray
Weather? I'll take apocrypha at its word and let them
Rise for an hour and glimmer, weakly, behind the clouds
I'm banking on. They bank in: The gray is almost uniform.

LINES WRITTEN AT TYRONE GUTHRIE: MAKING THE LOOP

The nose knows
before the eyes.
It makes meaning
before it spies
the honey locust,
the wild gorse,
the woodland spring;
inhales clean air
before the telly says
there's no pollution
in Ireland, or if there is,
it's washed clean by the sea.
The loop around the lake's
so fragrant green it fills
the brain with sights
before they're seen, more
memory than moment—
Scots pine, Irish yew,
Sessile oak, Sitka spruce,
from Dawson grove to
Anketell, the odors come.
And some smells are so old
they go back before the brawn
evolved to brain—back
when game was in the wind,
the nest egg in the canopy—
back when we were little
more than moss and duff
and all our senses snuffed
and touched through tendrils—
and back before when starfish
sensed the stars in salt, and
electric jolts of jellyfish touched
the cosmic minerals—
back when the sea was fresh.

STAIGUE FORT

Ireland, 5th century, A.D.

One hell of a world—
so circle stones five-men high
in Caherdaniel. Let stones curve between us
and the sun. Pile them far up a cirque
cupped in the hard hand of the mountain—
for we're all hard at it, bludgeoning each other
for a hectare of pasture carved from Gaelic rock.
Circle stones three-men wide. Wider than long
spears can pierce. If we survive, we can sail to stone
churches just off the coast, live a few peaceable years
past 25, those final years when a spear's heft
no longer pleases the hand. When a spear
and an arm become separate things.
One hell of a world on any knocknarea,
any hill of execution, in this country.
So pile stones high up a hillside.
Look down on invaders swarming
up the rocky valley, behind them
a foaming sea. Ready the spear points.
Crosscurrents pull the eye out, away,
swirling 10 miles to the Skelligs
where one-eyed Saint Finian, the leper monk,
has built from stone the last resort
of men, beehive huts, stony oratory,
and one great round-church in a monastery
high up on that high island, up among the nests
of stormbirds, gannet and petrel—but I know
of one bird, the shearwater, that builds no nest,
makes its egg pear-shaped and simply leaves it
on a ledge to balance in the wind. It's all
in the shape of the protection, the proportion
between the living thing and the stone
on which it suffers its siege.

WORTH

                                        Corte, Corsica

I sat on a high alpine hillside as the cuckoo
handed off the night to the scops owl
and estimated my worth to the world,
which wasn't much, wasn't really
the world's to consider. It was mine
and it was a heavy estimate
in the Corsican mountains with a glass
of local clementine spirits made by Paul
the local blowhard who shot his own
boars, milked his own goats,
made his cheese and honey and yes
these spirits I sat sipping under the alders
that were large and generous near his
hillside brook but dwarfed and stingy
on the high peaks where so little
was given or gotten. And the estimate
of my worth looked small indeed
to my eyes as deep twilight came on
and I could see so little until one by
one the stars showed me their lapsed
light from a billion years ago
and the scops owl sang all night
for nothing, for the sake of a mate
and his own sweet continuing.

LOCKDOWN IN LA CIOTAT, FRANCE

March-June, 2020

MARCH 14, 2020

We chose this working port long before Wuhan rhymed
with *quarantine*, Diamond Princess with *virus*. We chose it

for research work, the archives open to old accounts
of old France, its colonies conquered by force

and sickness, smallpox and syphilis—the virus
carried on their sailing ships. We chose it long before

we could predict the nature of our daily ruminations,
the nightmares they've become—the skewed sense of being

out of time. Now, archives closed, we haven't a chance
of concluding what we began in some unrestricted past.

Now we're all hostages of Blake's invisible worm as
it flies on the wind and finds *le nez, les yeux, la bouche*,

by which we take in the world and the world takes us out.
La Ciotat is, literally, The City—of handsome yachts,

of yachties who long ago longed to escape the land's curse
wafting from sweat shops, slaughterhouses, wild-game markets

to trouble their spars and sails. They're in for repairs,
then back out again, as soon as epoxy dries on their hulls.

For now, like us, they hunch at café tables, let the lull
of harbor waves lull them into false hopes that despair

lives elsewhere—in some well-contained sphere—they'll steer
clear of. Now they sterile-wipe a coffee cup for luck. No hearty shove

or backslap for a mate, no handshake. No kiss for one they love,
for love's sake. We sit nearby, a safe distance, imagine they're

mulling what we're mulling, the riddle of the virus:
We're all in this together, though we must stay apart,

for the sake of our lives floating on, for the sake
of recovering springtime, as if it needed us.

March 16, 2020: In a Blink

Last night stargazing here in La Ciotat,
I watched a few dim satellites drift over
and remembered their video feed of our
Earth's blue-green daytime with its white swirl
of clouds and remembered their night feed sweeping
over patches of world almost completely dark,
then larger swaths of twinkling lights, some seeming
almost to blink in isolation, some in clusters,
some in long unbroken skeins and rivers of light,
and some in knotted swarms so intense they seemed

like supernovas birthing new worlds from Earth.

Then I remembered why I was standing here
in darkness, with the cafés and clubs closed
down at the port, restaurants, cinemas,
casinos, all closed, and all the lights turned
off. And I imagined a new video feed
from a satellite eye that showed lights blinking
off around the world as the satellite followed
the curve of the Earth into unvarying darkness.
And I turned my gaze downward and followed
my footsteps home to the still-lit living room.

March 19, 2020

The numbers come closer even as people keep their distance.
The sick, the dying, the dead.
The numbers come closer to the county, the village, the streets
and houses surrounding us. Just
abstractions—for the sick are whisked away, while we walk in sunlight,
which is good for us, which kills
that which will kills us, and we move among the people
whom we move away from, lethal
potentials, virus vectors, good citizens all; let's be
kind, they desire what we desire, to breathe deep of the salt air.
And the numbers come closer.
We wander the old port dotted with tattoo shops and nail salons,
barbers and bookstores, all boarded up
under the shade trees, and we keep our distance
from those wandering similarly by,
a few handshakes apart, as chickadees dis-
appear into the holes
of blossoming redbuds, and bumblebees dis-
appear into the holes
of plane trees whose solid timbers the Greeks once used
to build their Trojan horse.

March 22, 2020: Lockdown Woman Working on a Tan

Downcast in these dying times, I wander
out into the quarantine, where each of us
must walk alone. A creaking shutter,
opening outward, causes me to see the canvas

of her back in the sun. It's March, she's pale,
the pandemic locks her in, so she pulls
the blue floor-to-ceiling windows open,
drops her morning robe to the marble floor,

and turns her long back and bony shoulders
to the almost-empty Place Émile Zola,
where this lone walker lifts his camera,
reads the light, adjusts the exposure,

and frames her on a bleak spring morning.
Her chamber's dark behind her, no telling
if a lover lies inside on a divan
or if she rose from a single bed alone.

She's the one object lit inside her room.
Outside, the sun intervenes, animating
the cobalt shutters, the wall's yellow-cream,
and begins its slow work of burning

her pale back to a canvas of resistance,
rousing, reddening against the pallor,
the lockdown, the floating invisible fear,
the harbor so quiet we hear the ripples slap

against boat hulls, wind worrying the clapper
against the bell in the empty church next door.
Floodlights hang on the winter-trimmed plane
trees, waiting for night's permission to shine,

as if their carbon beams could brighten
the gendarme's sign—*Fermé*—on every door.
The woman's back presses further toward the sun.
My camera eye reflects the burning there.

March 23, 2020

If one's daily walking meditations on the virus
unfold here,
                among the calanques of Côte d'Azur,
why not then learn from these
                        sunlit limestone cliffs

composed of the skeletal remains of sea creatures
and pebbled, cobbled conglomerate—
                        dashed
when rains and rivers washed through the porous
rock, opening, exposing,
                shaping into keyholes,
razorbacks, eagle beaks,
                      or in one dramatic
letting go, opening a clastic hillside into a cave.

Let the mind go where it goes—no need to remain
in the moment.
              Cast it far back and catch what lives
beneath this momentary surface.
                            Long ago,
(5 million years) during some catastrophe
we still don't understand—how it started, how it spread—
sea levels dropped
                dramatically (5,000 feet!)
and the Mediterranean was cut off
                        entirely
from the Atlantic.

In that geologic climate,
rains and rivers carved
                hundreds of feet into the Earth,
carrying away soil, eroding life forms, shaping

              the beauty to come
when after cycles of glacier and fissure the waters rose again
              and ocean poured in,

filling these canyons with water so clear
we could almost reach down and touch the ruins.

April 13, 2020

"My Foolish Heart" on YouTube, Bill Evans bent over
the keyboard, early '60s America, slicked-back hair
making him look older than he did days before his death,
and young Scott LaFaro leaning over the bass, unaware he'll be
tossed into roadside trees weeks from now,
the car speeding to a gig beyond double-time, out of
control, but now he's still, listening to Bill's solo,
plucking a few resonant bass notes of his own,
while Paul Motian brushes time against the skins.
Outside, empty streets, the virus chasing all of us
indoors to hide, to pass time listening to dead players
like Evans lay down tracks that live as long as
we're here to witness… which, lately, in this
vanishing time, seems tenuous, delicate as
Judas tree blossoms tossed in the final mistral
of the season that roared in last night, knocking out
power. Normally, that wind augurs a blue-sky ridge,
something that could accompany an unusually bright
D-minor ballad, say, "Bill's Hit Tune," or the straight-up
C-major of "Green Dolphin Street," but this morning,
it's not happening, it's not dazzling the Côte d'Azur
with sun that lifts us from the general dying. No, not today—
it's a rare thing, but it's blowing rain, and a lone figure,
struggling under a black umbrella says Bill should be
playing his plaintive ten-minute take on "Danny Boy."
Goddamn these rainy days. Only Evans, resurrected
before us in his holy-shouldered hunch, face turned,
cock-robin, to the keyboard, listening to sounds rise
from beneath his fingers that buzz the copper strings,
straining the rock-maple pin blocks that grip the tuning
keys so tight they'll never waver, could save us…
What the hell, it's spring, and my foolish heart
can't help itself—imagine Evans listening so intently
he hears the spruce soundboard, the maple bridges
and balsam-fir keys, the laminate overlay of mahogany
and rosewood, all communing and remembering their

tree-ness, how it was to sprout leaves, suck up soil minerals, sing through roots and root hairs to a whole underground community. Like us, perhaps, hoping to return to whatever our roots are, or were, hoping a virtual communing inside this high-tech box with Bill Evans inside it amounts to something, expressing us, our love of sound and touch, though many of us are sitting alone this morning, unsure of the day's death count, the long-term forecast.

April 15, 2020

Imagine all this time: a secret path
to the calanque's high cliffs—minutes
from home's stiff quarantine—
up a cul-de-sac, where the two
of us slip past gendarmes' traps,
clutching papers—just in case—certifying
we're a couple, not some interlopers
cleaving beyond social distancing,
though the tryst might do us
good in these lockdown times.
Uphill, the back gate opens
to the chatter of wagtail and rock
thrush, ushering in late-day light
with their inestimable bubble,
the wheeze of bee-eater and flycatcher,
singing, *here is the life we devour*,
all of them flitting amidst the Mediterranean
garrigue, where kermes oak and juniper
await the thunderbolt and propagating
fire that pops their seeds and cones
into the next green-birthing act,
and from there, they'll shade the scrub
of lavender and sage, while the sun
traces a path from North Africa over
Marseille, and onward to Gibraltar,
while two humans, escaped
from their compound, brush past
tufts of *gouffé* grass, bend
to sniff rosemary and thyme,
and wait for evening's shade
to bring out the cool vanilla smell
of gorse, bring down the free-
tailed bats from limestone overhangs,
the scops owl from its tree hole
to pierce evening with its siren mating call.

April 29, 2020

What a brilliant, blue-sky, Côte d'Azur day, roses
opening pink and yellow from the hedgerows,
joggers robust and red-faced on the back roads
huffing past my opened writing windows of the
repurposed horse stable where I rein in my wildness.
Why this blue weather battering my heart? I can't
stop counting the dying, can't stop accounting
for them one by one pouring over obits and pics
that bring them to rosy life again for the length
of a single reading before putting them back on ice
in the white semis humming outside the morgue.

∞

People are always bluing, aren't they, as Auden
intuited, while the rest of us go about our business.
But there's precious little business now except
virus business, those in the pink of health steady
in their white masks and green scrubs, growing
unsteady as they enter the ER doors to the legions
of the unresponsive, the intubated, the ventilated,
the induced comatose, the medically paralyzed,
the ones blue in the face, leaking exhausted blood
to machines that enliven it with oxygen, then pump
it back so they might, for another hour, breathe.

May 1, 2020: Labor Day in France

The figs are ripening, my neighbor Jumping John's
ratcheting up the trampoline for a lockdown
workout on Labor Day. His Aleppo pines,
from the oldest city in Syria, make their home here
in the warm mistral wind. Cultivated in the green sward
of his yard, his birds of paradise stick out their
orange-and-yellow tongues at poppies erupting
from sidewalk cracks, flaring from dirt lots
full of thistle and deadnettle, opium enough
for our neighborhood of cheek-to-jowl over-
and under-class to fill their work-free dreams.

MAPS.ME shows a blue swimming pool
in every third yard, no doubt family mansions, while
the two other habitations are former horse stables
repurposed for rent. Today, the smell of barbecue,
the hum of vacuums skimming holm oak leaves
from empty pools. And not far off,
a grating sound—maybe an ass braying
or a rooster pooped from relentless crowing
amidst the bitter vetch—keeps the laboring
sun from shining down with anything more
or less than brilliant indifference.

May 4, 2020

We inch closer to lockdown's end,
inch toward a line where the new
normal resides, wherever that is,
as it moves through days of light
and shadow, infections rise or abate,
abate or rise, and the line's redrawn.
Lilacs don't know this, their purple
clusters shamelessly luxurious, more
adventurous for having no gardener
tend them as they overhang the gate
and disperse their petals into the street,
where joggers stop, take off their masks,
and breathe the season's first mutations.

May 5, 2020

Every night at eight, boat horns blow from the old port:
low booms, long mid-register blasts, high-pitched sirens
rise from the Shipyards of La Ciotat, largest boat
restorer on the Côte d'Azur, where super-yachts are
hauled out of the sea with giant gantry cranes, hull
and keel cleaned, repaired, and set back into the drink;
where great sailboats float onto massive dry docks that swell
and drain while the boats settle for deep-gouge patch-ups,
refilled with fiberglass, brushed with gel, and buffed
back to health; and still others pull into the thousand
marina slips nearby to await renovations, living
on their ships, with the town in virus lockdown,
and they blow their horns each evening for the unseen,
the vanished, the unvanquished in their masks and gloves;

and my neighbors invisible beyond their walls
and hedgerows begin to clap, ring bells, blow car horns,
clank makeshift pots and pans, musical triangles,
and sad laughter fills the air crisscrossed by late-day swifts
and early evening bats, while a few plump mourning doves
startle from their low perch and flutter upward to
cypress and pine, while below, before doors close
on this diversion and the living return to aperitifs,
one hears sniffles or sobs, those who could be front-line
workers of hospitals and food shops, pharmacies and EMTs,
bus drivers, sanitation workers, all masked at sunup
to breathe the invisible viral air, unmasked
at sunset to leak away the day's dying tensions
with a kir royale, a bowl of nuts and salty olives.

May 13, 2020: End of Lockdown

Freshening winds off karst calanques lift
sea spray from the Mediterranean, shake out
tangled palms and cypresses, swoop down
to shiver purple heather and scoop up
vanilla scents of gorse, peppery thyme,
blow them through the opened windows
of La Ciotat this morning where we wake
to the first day of the end of lockdown.

We walk out onto streets free of attestations
noting our where, what for, and for how long,
free of gendarmes scribbling fines or cuffing
us for the station. Now we're free to drive
a hundred miles from home, to hike
hillside parks or make the pilgrim's circuit
to the Rock of Mercy itself, the grotto
of Sainte Baume, uplifted from the sea

an epoch ago, carved by erosion into caves
of deep sanctuary for the weary, as legend says,
all the way back to Magdalene and Lazarus.
Oh, we were weary of our lockdown,
the reliquary of our daily bread and wine,
the trespass of the virus in our pantries.
Oh, we were weary of those we loved,
our long-known and only society.

Now we wander hillsides and arrive
with anonymous others, masked, unmasked,
breathing the viral air together, hoping
the ventilated chambers of the church,
infused with savory breezes from outdoors,
reach us here and blow sweet release
through our sickened ranks now delivered
into the spreading palms of the day.

∞

CROWS IN SNOW

Johnson, Vermont

Out of snow-dark sky near sundown
flap the dark, ragged shapes of crows
tilting on squalls and gusts and sudden
pockets of stillness plunging toward
my iced windows, swooping upward again
pecking the necks of others in their pecking
order—or is it simply sheer, raucous play
that wings can shape the wind, tilt, swirl,
and two or three spin helixes almost
traceable against the sky and a murder
of ten or twenty suddenly storm the air
and hijack white blizzarding to black?

If, in this blizzard, the buzzing shapes
can do this, can I do this—shape
the black floating over white space,
play an identifying phrase against
erasure, weather a glum narrative,
spin a grander structure flapping upward
as crows go almost out of sight,
seeding clouds with dark intent and then, not—
just bursting through, like minor storm gods,
revealing how black transforms the gloom
of blizzarding sunset to a presence
almost luminous.

GRUDGING SPRING

Johnson, Vermont

And the fields green as old snows hiss
and dissipate in their last resistance
under maples in the north corner
of the pasture. And I'm stubborn, as
always, about stretching my limbs
toward the sun, surrendering this season
of reprieve from achievements, under-
written by pandemic's glacial pace.
This year, of all years, let the galas pale
or cancel their red carpets; let the stars,
the hopefuls, and hopeless rest under
the sublunary day-moon, while I rest on old
crusts of last year's storms, remember
blizzards that blinded me to the way forward,
recall how, in between squalls, sudden tracks
appeared in shapes of cleft hooves or
angel wings, sudden signposts arriving
only in a cold, fierce stillness that led to this
morning's maple buckets dripping
amber, this pasture's stubborn green.

ACKNOWLEDGMENTS

Poems from this book appear, sometimes in altered form, in the following publications:

A Poetry Congeries: "And Why Not Be Happy," "Cormorants in Full Sun," "Dad's Been Crying Again"
Big City Lit: "Milk, Eggs, Bread," "Under the Radar"
Birmingham Poetry Review: "Cezanne's Atelier"
Brilliant Corners: "Like Blue Behind a Daytime Moon," "Lockdown in La Ciotat: April 13, 2020," "Peacocks, for Evans," "So What," "That Sad Clapping"
The Common: "Lines Written at Tyrone Guthrie (Two hours rambling over gorse…)"
The High Window (England): "Questions for a Cormorant," "Lines Written at Tyrone Guthrie (Gray weather…)"
I-70 Review: "Lines Written at Tyrone Guthrie (I've seen one drifting…)"
LiVE Mag!: "How She Got That Voice"
Main Street Rag: "Going for a Drive"
Manhattan Review: "After the Blizzard," "Grudging Spring," "In the Vilnius Café," "Waves Going Out, Waves Coming In,"
Massachusetts Review: "There Is No Sadness"
Mudlark: "Crows in Snow," "Local Freeze"
New Verse News: "Big Winds"
Notre Dame Review: "Lines Written at Tyrone Guthrie (One more sunny day…)"
Rattle: "Lines Written at Tyrone Guthrie (Another day of slant rain…)"
Salmon Poetry Anthology (Ireland): "Lines Written at Tyrone Guthrie (The wind is up…)"
SALT: "Worth"
Sewanee Review: "Finifugal," "Staigue Fort"
Terrain.org: "End of August," "Late Fall," "Spring Poem, NYC"
Tikkun: "Exiles"
Two Horatios: "Lockdown in La Ciotat: May 4, 2020"
Vox Populi: "Mating Behaviors of Storks, Egrets, Humans," "Seagull in a Bowl"

Thanks to Jay White, Tony Whedon, Stephen Cramer, Terese Svoboda, Christine Gelineau, and Kate Riley, who read and commented on many of these poems and helped to make a stronger manuscript. Thanks to my editors, Kim Davis and Linda Parsons, whose expertise turned a manuscript into a beautifully edited and designed book. Thanks, lastly and always, to my wife, Kate Riley, and daughter, Anna Riley-Shepard, whose love and support undergird and sustain these creations.

ABOUT THE AUTHOR

Neil Shepard's eighth book of poetry, *How It Is: Selected Poems*, was published in 2018 by Salmon Poetry (Ireland), and in 2019 he edited *Vermont Poets & Their Craft* (Green Writers Press, VT). His previous poetry collections include *Hominid Up* (Salmon) and *Vermont Exit Ramps II* (GWP), both in 2015. His poems appear online at *Poetry Daily, Verse Daily* and *Poem-a-Day*, as well as in hundreds of literary magazines. He founded and edited for a quarter-century the *Green Mountains Review* and currently edits the online literary magazine *Plant-Human Quarterly*. These days, he splits his time between Vermont and NYC.